SPOOKY SAGAS

STORIES FROM THE SOUTH WEST

Edited By Jess Giaffreda

First published in Great Britain in 2019 by:

YoungWriters

Young Writers
Remus House
Coltsfoot Drive
Peterborough
PE2 9BF
Telephone: 01733 890066
Website: www.youngwriters.co.uk

Book Design by Ben Reeves

SB ISBN 978-1-78988-387-9
Printed and bound in the UK by BookPrintingUK
Website: www.bookprintinguk.com
YB0400R

FOREWORD

Welcome, Reader!

Here at Young Writers our aim is to encourage creativity in children and to inspire a love of the written word. Each competition we create is tailored to the relevant age group, hopefully giving each child the inspiration and incentive to create their own piece of work, whether it's a poem or a short story. We truly believe that seeing their work in print gives pupils a sense of achievement and pride.

For Young Writers' latest nationwide competition, Spooky Sagas, we gave primary school pupils the task of tackling one of the oldest story-telling traditions: the ghost story. However, we added a twist – they had to write it as a mini saga, a story in just 100 words!

These pupils rose to the challenge magnificently and this resulting collection of spooky sagas will certainly give you the creeps! You may meet friendly ghosts or creepy clowns, or be taken on Halloween adventures to haunted mansions and ghostly graveyards!

So if you think you're ready... read on.

CONTENTS

THE SPOOKY SAGAS

WHEN CHRISTMAS TURNED INTO HORROR HALLOWEEN!

It was the night before Christmas when Timmy heard a tapping noise coming from the basement.
"Mum, there is a terrible tapping noise coming from the basement!" yelled Timmy from his bed.
Weirdly, his mama didn't answer. *That's bizarre, she always answers,* thought Timmy.
He was curious so he wondered downstairs and there was a body lying on the carpet. She had blood dripping from her eyes. She had dark gruesome scars and wounds down her legs.
The strangest thing was her mouth, it was sewn together! Then zombies, vampires, wolves and more shot around the corner.
"Arghh!"

Brynleigh Rae Lewis (10)
Bridge Learning Campus, Hartcliffe

THE TALE OF THE ABANDONED THEME PARK

It was a dark and stormy night, a boy called Michael was at his friend, Fred's house when suddenly... *squeak!*
"The abandoned theme park!" they both said as they ran through the door.
When they got there, they heard... *Burr! Whoosh! Squeak!* As they ran to the roller coaster, they noticed the noises were getting louder.
"Help!" called Fred. "Help me!"
As Michael ran to save Fred, he saw Fred's skin was green!
"Burrr!" said Fred.
Michael ran to his house and thought about what he was going to do.

Jayden Martain Adam Plaster (10)
Bridge Learning Campus, Hartcliffe

THE LOCKDOWN

Ben's hands clenched his sweaty face as the bell rang. A lockdown. Then at once, the thief flew into the school and started testing each and every door but they were locked. As quickly as possible, Ben locked himself in his locker and realised he couldn't get out. Then he looked through a hole in the locker and saw the robber peel off his mask and behind was a horrid, green, flesh-eaten face. Unexpectedly, the robber entered Charlie's classroom and all Ben heard was *bang, bang, bang!* Tears welled in his eyes... Charlie had been killed. Only Ben remained...

Jayd Parker (10)
Bridge Learning Campus, Hartcliffe

THE MYSTERIOUS SCREAMS

As the blinding moon rose, Shadow, a courageous girl with sapphire-blue coloured eyes and purple hair took a step into the forest and...
Screams! There were screams coming from every direction and her friends that used to be at the gate were gone! They couldn't have left her all alone, they *couldn't* have! The screams were getting louder and louder so she ran and ran until... Everything was ink-black. All she heard were the screams. There were hands on her.
Finally, she saw them, black figures, they screamed. Suddenly, she was gone...

Natalie Szczesna (10)
Bridge Learning Campus, Hartcliffe

THE FIRE STARTER

The ashes came before the fire. All that was left was the smell of smoke and dust. How the flat burnt was a mystery to the world. All everyone knew was that there was a bottle of gasoline, a lighter and a body...
"Why did you do it?" a voice screamed in Jim's ear.
"Answer me!" it screamed and bellowed until Jim screamed himself.
He wasn't asleep so this couldn't be a dream. It was a dream-like illusion close to reality.
Later that night, the voice came again. It sounded like his daughter, who he killed in the fire...

Gracie Andreoletti (11)
Bridge Learning Campus, Hartcliffe

STRANGE THINGS

On the eve of Halloween, there was a strange girl roaming around, who went into a quiet church.
Suddenly, a huge, light blue haze covered the entire graveyard! Strange things started to happen, black figures started to come out of the dark brown ground, moaning and groaning could be heard from miles away.
Behind the girl was a secret door so she went in to explore. Little did she know, it would teleport her to a different world.
At the bottom of the stairs, were three openings. She decided to go through number three, then something grabbed her leg...

Courtney Smith (11)
Bridge Learning Campus, Hartcliffe

THE ABANDONED GRAVEYARD

On Bishop Road, there lived three teenagers: Sarah, Lacy and Matt.
One day, they all decided to go and visit the abandoned graveyard.
The next evening, they all travelled there and Lacy saw one of her relation's graves. She started to cry.
Suddenly, they all heard a powerful scream that rang through their ears. They were intimidated by the sound. It was pitch-black. All of a sudden, thick fog appeared and something brushed Lacy's shoulder. It felt like a freezing hand. Lacy turned around to see what it was but it had vanished into thin air!

Lily-Mae Ford (10)
Bridge Learning Campus, Hartcliffe

OUR TERRIBLE MISTAKE

In the year 2072, Professor Winconton created a black hole whilst doing an experiment. People around the world saw a beaming light in the sky. The beaming light began to grow bigger and bigger...
Suddenly, NASA detected five ships in our atmosphere. Strange-looking creatures fell from the ships and landed in Flanders Fields. Professor Winconton zoomed in to the creatures and discovered they were zombies. He warned the army and had to prepare for a human vs zombie war! Who would win? The fate of the world was in our hands, we decided who would win or lose.

Joshua Heathcote Davies (10)
Bridge Learning Campus, Hartcliffe

THE MYSTERIOUS MAN

One bright, sunny day, Charlie was sent out to collect the corn so he could have a nice, juicy corn on the cob with butter. It started to get dark and foggy. Shivers fell down his spine. He looked behind him - nothing. He turned back around - still nothing. He started to collect the long, yellow corn. It got gloomier and gloomier. He looked beside him. A faint, dark figure appeared in front of him. It got closer and closer until he could see the darkness in his eyes. Almost unbelievably, he disappeared... Suddenly, a rough-edged stick brushed against his face.

Harley Clark (10)
Bridge Learning Campus, Hartcliffe

THE TWO BOYS AND THE GHOST

It was 30th October, 2.59am and the two boys, Noah and Lucus, were in the abandoned house. They were exploring to see if ghosts were real. Were they?
As Lucus kept taking more steps up the stairs, Noah kept hearing noises but Lucus thought he was lying. Although he really wasn't!
Noah kept crying, "I want to go home!"
Lucus just ignored him though.
Noah tried to find the window he came through but he got lost. Suddenly, he heard a creepy noise. It sounded like a witch's laugh. Was it Lucus? He didn't know... or did he?

Alfie Mills (10)
Bridge Learning Campus, Hartcliffe

ANNABELLE'S ROAD TO SAFETY

Annabelle went to get her lunch from her locker.
Back in the cafeteria, Annabelle realised everyone was gone. She wandered around to see if anyone had been sent to a room but no one was in the school. All around her were voices. Annabelle ran to the door but it was locked. The voices were getting louder...
They were saying, "If you obey our instructions, you will be free!"
All she had to do was to forgive her mum about lying about her sister. Annabelle rang her mum and apologised to her. The doors opened and she ran to safety...

Grace Stokes (11)
Bridge Learning Campus, Hartcliffe

THE HORROR IN THE SUBWAY

It was pitch-black outside and Max was in the subway. All of a sudden, something brushed against his cheek. The lights flickered on, off, on, off constantly. Everything went cold. A loud echo travelled the room.

"He he he!" it giggled.

Max gasped and shivered in terror. In the blink of an eye, he had fallen to the cold, hard ground. The giggling got closer now, closer, closer and then... *zoom!* A train sped by and when it had passed, Max had vanished. He was never, ever seen again until the day that was named Halloween.

Elle-May Lester (10)
Bridge Learning Campus, Hartcliffe

ON HALLOWEEN NIGHT

One Halloween night, Lucy asked if she could visit her father's grave, so then she strode into the ghostly, haunted graveyard. She found her dad's grave, then she stepped closer and stared at it, thinking of all the wonderful memories they had and what he taught her when she was young.

Then all of a sudden, she heard a stick snap. She didn't want to turn around but then she felt a horrible hand on her shoulder. She looked at the hand and was about to scream. She looked quickly around and ran from the zombie...

Destiny Donaldson (11)
Bridge Learning Campus, Hartcliffe

PING-PONG IS DEADLY

It was five years ago when Bob's dad died.
Every Sunday, he went to visit his grave but this time was very, very deadly.
When he was about to leave, he saw a strange figure in the mist.
"Hello?" said Bob cautiously.
Nobody replied.
"Arghh!" screamed Bob.
A rock-hard ping-pong ball hit him in the face. *What is it? Could it be? It couldn't be...* It was Harley C, a world champion ping-pong player... but he died one hundred years ago.
Bob was never seen again.

Chase Bloomfield (10)
Bridge Learning Campus, Hartcliffe

THE NIGHT BEFORE HALLOWEEN

As darkness approached the world, it was time to do our test, until... the lights flickered, all of a sudden it went pitch-black. The whole class screamed at the top of their lungs. Nerves slowly shivered up my body. The bright lights turned back on. The teacher was nowhere to be seen. The whole class searched for her but she wasn't there.
The whole school sprinted outside as they screamed in horror. In the blink of an eye, the school was gone, it was like it never happened. I never saw it again...

Millie Farrell (10)
Bridge Learning Campus, Hartcliffe

STITCHES SEW DEEP

My heart battered my ears as I forced my breath back down into my deflated lungs. We all knew what it was and somehow, it knew us. The fog started to clear and a faint outline arose from in-between the smudged trees. It became clear that this thing was not, or if it was, barely, human. It had a sewn outline and looked like it was made from a potato sack. My hands floated to my mouth to cover a gaping hole in my face, plugging it so not a word could come out. It was Stitched Mouth...

Ruby Hann (10)
Bridge Learning Campus, Hartcliffe

JASON AND MARY TEAM UP

On Friday 13th, the full moon was out and a boy called Georgie was in a camp bedroom. He woke up from a nightmare and he wanted to clear his head so he went to the bathroom. He threw water onto his face and looked up. He saw a person with long hair! He looked behind him and no one was there. He looked at the mirror, then he closed his eyes and opened them... she was still there and she had a friend with a machete! He looked back again and they weren't there. Was it a dream?

Zack Swatton (10)
Bridge Learning Campus, Hartcliffe

ZOMBIE PUMPKINS

Wendy the witch was feeling very naughty so she put a zombie spell on all her pumpkins in her pumpkin patch. At Halloween, the pumpkins were sold for pumpkin carving. Unfortunately, Ewan the unicorn and Flora the fairy bought one!
Later on, during their Halloween party, the pumpkin started to grow bigger and bigger until all the guests were squished against the walls. Suddenly, the enormous zombie pumpkin exploded! Pumpkin juice and seeds covered everyone, but worst of all, they turned into zombies!
The zombies ran all around the town, trick or treating, making everyone scream and some people faint!

Rachel Doig (7)
Charter Primary School, Chippenham

VICTOR'S SCARE

Victor looked like a normal boy. His friends came for a creepy party. They wore scary costumes! The food looked yummy, there were chocolate spiders and jelly worms! They were having lots of fun and were dancing to a scary disco when suddenly, the windows blew open and ghosts flew in!
Everyone screamed and when they looked at the food, it was wriggling and crawling! The ghosts were Victor's mum and dad! Victor was a ghost too! He turned invisible and all his friends turned and ran out of the house, screaming. Victor flew after them. He was very sad!

Morgan Taylor (7)
Charter Primary School, Chippenham

THE MYSTERY CLUE

Once upon a time, there was a witch's castle and dripping blood. Creepily, it had whispering voices and moving objects. The witch got closer and she went downstairs. She wondered what it was. She soon figured out the moving objects was her pet ghost moving them and the whispering voices was Mum on the phone, but wait... there was something else! It was lumbering and tall, it was her brother and sister but they just wanted the best Halloween ever. They danced and sang spooky songs. After, they went back to bed. Good fright!

Lola Maxwell (7)
Charter Primary School, Chippenham

GEORGE AND THE CREAKY DRAWER

George is fast asleep in his soft, cosy bed, really happy as he has just eaten a delicious ham pizza. Suddenly, there is a loud, creaky noise. George wakes up startled. He switches on the light and notices in the corner of the room, covered in cobwebs and spiders, a drawer is open. Just as he is about to close the drawer, it releases an old, dusty pen into the air. George is frozen to the spot with his mouth wide open. The pen hovers as it writes on the wall in scribbled handwriting: 'I'm watching you!'

Oliver Gray (8)
Charter Primary School, Chippenham

BOB'S CAUGHT SOMETHING STRANGE

Down in the cellar lived Bob the spider. He had been busy making a beautiful web to catch his food. He saw that he had caught something! Excitedly, he climbed the web and saw a very strange, green, dirty thing looking at him.
He said he was Bogey the Goblin! Bob saw Bogey do horrifying things! Bogey used his earwax to style his hair, he picked his nose and ate it! Bogey rubbed his feet all over his dinner to make it taste cheesy! Bob felt that Bogey was too disgusting to eat and let him go.

Sophia Doig (7)
Charter Primary School, Chippenham

SILVIA THE VAMPIRE AND THE HILL

One spooky night a long time ago, there lived a vampire called Silvia. She lived on the spookiest hill where bad things lived. Silvia was a good vampire but sometimes got into trouble!
One day, she was on her way home when she saw a strange figure. She saw it run, then heard a loud noise. *Bang!* She jumped in fear and changed into a bat. She turned around, it looked massive, scary and had big, sharp razor teeth! She saw the reflection but it was only her little cat, Roxie...

Poppy Jenkins (7)
Charter Primary School, Chippenham

THE MYSTERIOUS THEME PARK

It was 3am when Peter, George and Billy were hunting for ghosts when suddenly, they heard the sound of mechanical parts screeching together. They turned around and saw a deserted theme park that was billowing smoke out of the gates. Billy had a horrific look on his face. Seeing this, George dared Billy to go in.
"No!" he screamed.
"Well, a dare's a dare!" Peter explained.
"Fine," Billy muttered as he walked through the gates.
Soon, he disappeared.
Soon after, a loud bang could be heard and Billy screamed, "Help!"
Ashes and bones flew through the gates.
"Help me!"

Peter Evan James Carew (10)
Dobwalls Community Primary School, Dobwalls

CIARAN'S HOSPITAL HORROR

Ciaran shook with fear. After all, Fin dared him to go to an abandoned hospital. No wonder he was scared!

They arrived.

"The door's blocked," said Ciaran.

Fin got a crowbar and ripped down the doors. They explored the four floors. Suddenly, outside, they heard an ambulance.

"It's probably a ghost or something," Fin added.

Ciaran whispered, "Let's continue!"

They walked down the hall. The light turned off and flickered on. Fin was gone... Ciaran went running. He checked on all floors. He went outside.

"Boo!" Fin screamed. "I planned this out!" he laughed.

Ciaran Anthony John Thomas (10)
Dobwalls Community Primary School, Dobwalls

HIDE-AND-SEEK

Anthony finally woke, darkness and fear overcame him as his eyes adjusted. He looked around to find the front door. Anthony sat bolt upright and ran to the door, desperately trying to open it. Just then, Anthony, to his horror, heard loud and ominous footsteps behind him.
"Who's there?" Anthony stuttered.
When he went to turn around, Anthony realised nobody was there. Suddenly, a door slammed and scared Anthony out of his skin. Rapid footsteps upstairs started coming closer and soon they'd started coming down the stairs. Anthony couldn't find a place to hide.
"Finally, I have found you..."

Silas Sutton (11)
Dobwalls Community Primary School, Dobwalls

THE UNKNOWN

Clutching the handle of her suitcase, Ashleigh's blue eyes widened as they saw the magnificent hotel. Shyly, she entered. The receptionist gave her her key. After unpacking most of her belongings, she crawled under her duvet and slept. She awoke, something was different. Sitting up, Ashleigh's golden hair slid down her back. Eyes glancing, she walked out the door. She froze to the spot. There was a girl who was humming a song, tilting her head like a pendulum, with black holes for eyes, like another dimension was coming closer.
Everything went black...
A deep voice laughed, "You can't escape!"

Kess Davies (10)
Dobwalls Community Primary School, Dobwalls

THE REFLECTION

Snow pattered against Edward's bedroom window, casting morphing shadows on his mattress. An uneasy feeling began to stir inside the boy, so with a click, he turned on his light. However, this sinister sensation only seemed to worsen, spreading throughout his body like a snake.

At that moment, it bit him, not causing pain, but blackening Edward's vision for a heartbeat. Then light swarmed back in, destroying Edward's panic. Edward relaxed for a moment, then his blood ran cold for his mirror had smashed. In its place was his reflection, but it wasn't his reflection anymore, it was real...

Gregory Welsh (10)

Dobwalls Community Primary School, Dobwalls

THE PYRAMID OF DEATH

Glistening rubies, sapphires and emeralds lay before Archie. Delighted, he went inside when... *Bang!* The door slid shut.
Soon after, the lid on Tutankhamun's sarcophagus swung open, revealing a terrible, horrific sight. Inside lay the body of his wife. In a flash, her eyes opened and she screamed for help. Before he could speak, she had been sucked into the wall. He fell to his knees with anger and depression. Tutankhamun walked up to Archie who was oblivious to what was happening and placed his hand on Archie's shoulder. Archie screamed and never saw daylight again...

Grace Stephanie Dunn (11)
Dobwalls Community Primary School, Dobwalls

THE WOODS

This all started on Halloween when a rich girl named Sasha moved into a mansion with her friend Riley and her best friend, Amy. Amy and Sasha started vampire school together. Riley went to ghost school.
A few years later, when Sasha and Riley came back from Christmas shopping, there was a note from Amy on the fridge saying: 'I'll be back late!' written in blood.
Sasha and Riley woke up the next morning, Amy still wasn't home. Sasha went to the woods to find Amy. Amy screamed.
Sasha shouted, "Amy!"
No one answered. Sasha went home in tears.

Amy Lane (10)
Dobwalls Community Primary School, Dobwalls

SPOOKY ROOM!

Last Wednesday, we were at school and it all started with truth or dare. We chose dare, so suddenly we were in a rundown theme park about to step inside a tent called 'Spooky Room'. The letters were a little faded but we could see them.
Once inside, there were other people walking around clockwise. Slowly, we walked up to a man.
"Excuse me, but what are you doing?" He didn't reply but took us to a small, dark room. Then he turned around and left us.
Someone spoke, "We have been expecting you!"
Suddenly, there was just silence...

Sienna Brewer (11)
Dobwalls Community Primary School, Dobwalls

THE MINE OF SOULS

It was a dark and misty night. It was 1am and it was windy.
When George and Peter were playing football, the ball rolled down near a mine and George spotted it and shouted to Peter. They both spotted a ladder and went down. They saw human souls. Suddenly, a loud bang and a trap door appeared. George saw a jar, it had names of people who were going to die. Suddenly, they heard a laugh. Peter felt something running over his shoulder.
There was a voice saying, "I've been waiting for you..."
George felt something run through his hair...

Billy Saxon Cullingford (11)
Dobwalls Community Primary School, Dobwalls

BLACK EYES

It was nine o'clock at night. Taylor and Riley were getting ready to go to the Halloween party. When they were ready, they took a shortcut through the woods.
When they got there, they walked in but no one was there. They were confused because it started at eight o'clock and finished at ten o'clock. It was nine o'clock! Riley kept groaning and kept saying he saw black figures and repeatedly saying he felt sick.
Five minutes later, a bench threw itself at us, but particularly at me. It missed. Riley's eyes were jet black. He was possessed.

Taylor James Lee Trebilcock (10)
Dobwalls Community Primary School, Dobwalls

THE LOOMING PRESENCE

The pilot could feel the presence of a shadow lurking behind him. Yet he still focused on his task to safely deliver the passengers. The pilot could feel a soft scratch on his nape. Unaware of what he might find, he swivelled around on his chair but nothing was there, the pilot stood up and searched.
Flick! All the lights turned off. The passengers gathered around and started shrieking, asking what had happened. They went up to question the pilot. Suddenly, the bulb switched on. The cabin was calm, until the light shone on the clammy body of the pilot.

Finlay Dunn (11)
Dobwalls Community Primary School, Dobwalls

THE UNFORGETTABLE EVENING

Zendaya and Zac on their way home came across an abandoned school.
"I dare you to go in!" Zendaya said.
Not trying to be a wimp, Zac agreed to enter. While heading in, lights flickered in the corridor. Without a second to lose, they came across an old hall full of smashed glass. Everything was silent, no one in sight, then out of the blue, *bang!* What was going on? Zac went to turn around and Zendaya was gone. All that was left was her cold, dark hair. Then came a voice from behind Zac.
"Well, you came too."

Emily Heather Collings (10)
Dobwalls Community Primary School, Dobwalls

HALLOWEEN!

One spine-chilling Halloween night, Riley and Jaden were thinking of costumes to wear, when someone knocked on the door. It was a trick-or-treater dressed as half-boy, half-wolf. Riley and Jaden decided it was a good idea, so they went trick or treating.
When they stepped outside they saw a light coming from the house everyone thought was haunted, so they went to look.
When they got to the door, a cold, tingly feeling ran down their spines. Just then, a tall, skinny shadow swooped past the window. Then the wooden door creaked slowly open...

Riley Pownall (10)
Dobwalls Community Primary School, Dobwalls

THE GLITCH

An unknown boy gamed. He would never stop. One day, in his little town, the boy was playing a horror game. Sadly, he was addicted. Then the explosive lightning glitched his game. He was annoyed! He started screaming and shouting until there was a *tap, tap, tap!* A scraping was heard at the battered window. *Screech!* In a split second, the boy spun around on his chair. Nothing was there... *Bang!* His window shattered, spraying glass all over the floor. The blank-faced man was there...
The boy was never seen again...

Tarryn John Mollard (10)
Dobwalls Community Primary School, Dobwalls

THE OLD FANTASTIC FUNFAIR

Me, Grace and Sienna ran to the snow-covered sign which said: *Fantastic Funfair!*
In the fair, all the rides were covered in snow. When we went to the funhouse, a man asked us to follow. We did. He took us to another fair. When we arrived, it got colder. Only one light was on - the Ferris wheel. Mysteriously, he showed us on. It started moving, but stopped at the top. Beginning to panic, I looked at Sienna. She had no shadow. Without warning, it got colder. I could hear the snow, then I heard a shivering scream...

Sierra Jones (11)
Dobwalls Community Primary School, Dobwalls

I'VE BEEN EXPECTING YOU

Jake was wandering around the woods. In the corner of his eye, he found a hut. Jake walked to the door, he found it was locked. With fury, he bashed on the door and walked away. It creaked open. Jake ran through the door and fell down a hole into water. Jake finally got out the hole and followed the path. All you could see was a light getting lighter. Eventually, he got to the end. There was a shelf of pots and one was empty with his name on.
Suddenly, he heard a voice saying, "I've been expecting you..."

Ollie Andrew McVeigh (10)
Dobwalls Community Primary School, Dobwalls

THERE WAS A HAND

Last Thursday, I was at school and had just started and I had made new friends, Sasha, Jessy, Jade and Perry, but Sasha and Perry came back to my house. We went in the attic and we went under the bed in the attic. Sasha screamed!

I shouted, "What's wrong?"

I turned around and she disappeared. Then I turned back around, there were Perry and Sasha on the bed, frightened. There was a hand on the bed so we all screamed the loudest we could but it disappeared, so did Sasha and Perry.

Kiera Varcoe (11)
Dobwalls Community Primary School, Dobwalls

THE HAUNTED NIGHT

Matt woke up with a bang. He didn't know what woke him up. As quiet as a mouse, he looked around his room. Matt heard floorboards creaking. He saw shadows around the room. As scared as a mouse, he ran to his bed and hid under the covers. He heard a bang under his bed... he looked under and saw a girl with red eyes!
He screamed and the little girl said, "I'm coming for you!"
Just then, she disappeared with a smile. In horror, the boy was paralysed and then he fainted...

Jimi Hancock (11)
Dobwalls Community Primary School, Dobwalls

THE DEATH EATERS

It was a dark and stormy night. The sky was grey and black. Marly was snuggled up in bed whilst snuggling Bunny. Suddenly, there was something banging on the door. *Bang!* Marly crept underneath her bed. Shivers went down her back. The door handle creaked and someone opened the door. Someone was in the room. Marly turned her head and screamed because a bony head peered at her.
That was the night of Marly's death but she still comes and creeps around the haunted house...

Marly Gray (10)
Dobwalls Community Primary School, Dobwalls

THE MONSTER TRICK OR TREAT

Ding dong! went the doorbell.
"I'd better go and answer that," Alex said to herself.
Moments later, she was outside, ready to hand out sweets, but it wasn't what she thought it was. As the trick-or-treater came closer, Alex noticed that it was not a trick-or-treater, but actually a *monster!* Alex ran inside and grabbed the first thing she saw - a jar of pickled onions. Soon, Alex was outside throwing pickled onions at a monster.
After five minutes of pickled onion-throwing, the monster was on the floor, melting.
"Boo-yah!" yelled Alex as she strolled inside triumphantly.

Iris Hutton (9)
Emersons Green Primary School, Emersons Green

VAMPIRE ON THE RUN

One dark and stormy night, I was talking to my friend about the abandoned wood.
"I'm not scared!" I pleaded.
"Fine, go there then!"
"Okay!" I said.
Afterwards, I set off to the wicked wood.
When I got there, a dark figure stood in front of me. Worst of all, he had fangs! Freaky deeky! Getting scared, I ran away. I ran and ran and ran! He was still chasing after me! What to do? Still chasing me, I screamed and screamed and screamed. He finally caught me to bite, only to realise that it was Halloween.
"Trick or treat!"

Sanah Azhar (10)
Emersons Green Primary School, Emersons Green

EMRALDO AND THE HAUNTED CASTLE

One Halloween night, Emraldo and his brothers and sisters slowly walked into a pitch-black haunted castle. As soon as they walked in, they heard an ear-piercing smash in the darkness before them. They froze. They heard something scutter along the cold, damp floor. They heard a long, slow screech. They ran towards the light.

Once they were in, the doors screeched their long, slow screech. The lift said it was going down 5,000 miles into the Earth. They found a hatch and escaped just in time!

"Let's never do that again!" said Emraldo!

They ran all the way home.

Jack Bishop (9)

Emersons Green Primary School, Emersons Green

THE TWOSOME GRUESOME

Under the midnight moon, when the sun was no longer awake, two blood-dripping werewolves lay watching their dinner for the night. With their open jaws and staring eyes, it was obvious that they were ready to catch their prey. Quickly and quietly, they set off but behind them, there was something that stopped them dead in their tracks.
It slowly walked over to them and said one gruesome word, then wandered off, but threateningly muttered to itself, "I'll be back to teach them a lesson!"
Then silence was held amongst the autumn woods and the moon began to fall.

Megan Eatwell (9)
Emersons Green Primary School, Emersons Green

ETERNAL DARKNESS

As the class scuttled into the foyer, Taylor could smell the foul odour of rats. Stepping down into the dark, claustrophobic dungeon with his dad behind him, he felt a shiver down his spine. As he continued, he became aware that the class had moved on without him. Suddenly, he heard subtle whispering voices, "Taylor follow us, follow!"
Immediately, a grotesque face and an arm as slippery as a snake burst out of the wall and pulled Taylor's dad into the brickwork. He turned back to find his dad had disappeared. Would Taylor ever see his dad's face again?

Evan Michael Gard (10)
Emersons Green Primary School, Emersons Green

SPOOKY HAPPENINGS

I live in an ordinary house and my name is Amy.
Walking into my bedroom, I got into bed and closed my eyes.
"Hello, Amy," said a strange voice.
I sat straight up and rushed to the bathroom quickly to splash myself with cold water. When I looked into the vast sink, I could see an eyeball staring straight at me. Running into the hallway, screaming loudly, I could see a black, hooded figure walking towards me. I ran into my room, slamming the oak door and hid, shaking.
The door opened and the hooded figure walked in...

Lucy Budd (10)
Emersons Green Primary School, Emersons Green

KILLER CAR KID

Once upon a creepy night, Mangotsfield School was open for a sleepover night. All of class 5-F were staying there that night but something was different... One by one, a student would go to the loo and then nothing. The kid wouldn't come back. For one particular reason, they were being killed! By who, you might wonder. It was the legendary Killer Car Kid!

One foolish kid named Bertie went to the loo and he saw the killer kid's killer car eating the last juicy morsel and then, Bertie didn't notice that the car knew he was there.

Dan Britton (11)
Emersons Green Primary School, Emersons Green

THE HAUNTED MANOR

One morning, Matthew played in his garden but out of nowhere, a portal opened up and Matthew fell in! He returned out in a disturbingly weird manor. The manor looked like it had not been tidied for centuries! Suddenly, a creak came from the floor. The walls began to vibrate. The door slowly moved open. Matthew hid in the corner. From the door came a zombie which looked like something had taken a large bite out of it. Matthew screamed with horror! He leapt back into the portal. Matthew was safe... well, he *thought*...

Thomas Manning (11)
Emersons Green Primary School, Emersons Green

THE ALIEN

Jim signed up to be a Monster Hunter so he could see exquisite creatures, not *kill* them. But that all changed when he arrived at the space station. Instead of seeing life, he only saw death! It was horrible!
Now Jim was determined to kill the thing. A shadow moved past Jim. He pointed the killer at the shadow and fired like a madman. When he opened his eyes, Jim realised that he'd just shot an innocent person but he had no time to feel sad about it. As he turned, he saw pitch-black. Jim had been killed.

Cai F Owen Herrero (10)
Emersons Green Primary School, Emersons Green

THE NIGHT TERROR

Once upon a time, a blonde-haired boy was walking along the road when he came across an old house. It was a scary but small house. The walls were painted pitch-black. Then the small boy decided to have a look in the house, so he did. A few seconds later, it struck midnight. The moon was bright.
After that, a portal opened so the boy went in. Then he appeared in a forest. It was dark and spooky there and the moon was bright. Silently, a crunch in the leaves. Behind him stood a dark, furry shape, grinning angrily.

Josh Eatwell (9)
Emersons Green Primary School, Emersons Green

SAM HEARS CREEPY NOISES

Off I went to the dark, creepy house. I walked in to find a man sitting in the dark. The chair was creaking and there were cobwebs everywhere. I turned around because I could feel a cool breeze on the back of my neck. I couldn't see anyone but I could hear a faint whisper.
It sounded like, "Hey, Sam, is that you, boy?"
When I turned back, the man in the chair was gone. I walked around the house a little, I was feeling very frightened!
I decided it was best I left, so off I ran home!

Alfie Phillips (10)
Emersons Green Primary School, Emersons Green

DASH'S CRAZY MORNING

It was one normal morning and Dash had just woken up. He was putting on his monster slippers and getting dressed until he heard a noise.
"Hello?" said Dash, but there was no reply...
Then he looked closer and he saw long, sharp nails and a black, long dress. Dash tried to scream but nothing came out. Then his mum came and the shadow and Dash were gone. His mum was really worried! She looked downstairs, upstairs but she couldn't find him. Suddenly, when she got back, he was there!

Olivia Bennett Baradad (9)
Emersons Green Primary School, Emersons Green

SPOOK MEETS ME!

I woke up. Where was I? All I could see was darkness and one door covered in dragon's blood. The ceiling was broken. I looked up and could see a tall, thin, stick-like figure. A clock struck midnight in the distance. I felt myself burning white. What was happening? Was I a ghost, like all my family were? Why? Why?
I looked at myself in some broken piece of glass. I was... I was a ghost like my whole family now! I looked up at the figure. It was my older brother, George, trying to scare me! Why?

Ella Wilson (9)
Emersons Green Primary School, Emersons Green

BETTER WATCH OUT, SLIME EVERYWHERE

One stormy night in the attic, a boy went up to read but then he saw a dark, drooping figure walking towards him, leaving a slimy trail.
Ethan suddenly ran around the attic until he tripped. He tried to call his mum or dad but he realised they were asleep. The figure then started to peel its slimy head, then its body!
Fearfully, Ethan looked closer and saw it was his dad! It was Halloween and Ethan had forgotten!
In the morning, he woke up with a start. He felt like it was just a dream, or was it?

Sabah Azhar (8)
Emersons Green Primary School, Emersons Green

TRICK OR TREAT!

One night, when I was trick or treating, I came across a house.
When I knocked on the door, it opened. I went in and all I could see was blackness. I realised, out the corner of my eye, I could see a bowl of sweets. I went over to them and grabbed a couple of sweets. Suddenly, a ghost flew right through me. Then a vampire turned into a bat and flew over my head! Then I heard a big, laughing voice. It was Mum and Dad saying how scared I was made them laugh.
"Tricked you!" they said.

Amelia Jorja Bradbury (10)
Emersons Green Primary School, Emersons Green

THE SWALLOW UP HOUSE

In a small city, there's a scary house that eats you up if you dare to go on its path. It's actually not an ordinary path. It is actually a gritty tongue that pulls you in if you go on it.
In the house, a filthy witch hates for kids to dare to go on the grey, gritty tongue.
One day, a boy called Ben goes on it and gets pulled in. She turns him into a scary, green zombie! Then he bites somebody, then he bites somebody else and then zombies own the whole wide world!

Kai Matthew Hurley (8)
Emersons Green Primary School, Emersons Green

THE CLOWN

There once was a clown. He was going trick or treating. He went to the end of the road where his clown friend called Sam lived. He and his friend went to the forest. They got kidnapped by a ghost! They were so scared.
Sam said, "Hello, ghost!"
The ghost disappeared and a vampire appeared from a wall. It was a very haunted house so we ran back to Sam's house and hid behind a chair. The ghost came in too, so did the vampire. They just wanted to play together!

Maisie Reeves (8)
Emersons Green Primary School, Emersons Green

ZOOMING ZOMBIES

Once there lived a zombie called Zombilina who loved scaring people. There was only one thing, she had no friends because they didn't like scaring people and now I'm going to tell you her story.
One day, Zombilina was in a school scaring people. On Tuesday, her dad told her to stop scaring people and she listened. She made lots of friends all around the world! Now she wasn't lonely, but really popular most of the time. She still scared her teacher though.

Noah Bennett (9)
Emersons Green Primary School, Emersons Green

HAUNTED HOUSE

There's a house monster in my house and there's a scary baby. My house is haunted. Sometimes I shut my eyes as it helps me to feel safe. Keep safe and don't come near my house. You have been warned! You must keep away! Please don't tell anyone my house is haunted. If you do, the house monster will kill people. You should be afraid of me. I have warned you so you know not to come near me.

Lili Moorman (10)
Emersons Green Primary School, Emersons Green

HAPPY HALLOWEEN!

I'm trapped. I'm trapped in a petrifying house! I could see black figures creeping on the cracked walls. I could smell gloopy slime which has slugs! I could hear loud, horrid noises coming closer every second. I could feel hairy spiders tickling under my toes.
Is this a nightmare or is this real? I could see scraped walls which had dull paintings.
A voice suddenly said, "Come, come, come a little closer!" Horrifyingly, I took one small step forward. "Come closer!"
I went closer.
"Come closer!"
This time I was shivering and took three steps forward.
"Come! Happy Halloween!"

Mahasin Fathima Mohamed Rafi (9)
Even Swindon Primary School, Raybrook Park

THE WHISPERING HALLOWEEN

Many moons ago, on a moonlit night, a group of trick-or-treaters came across an old, abandoned house. As they got closer, they heard peculiar, grotesque whispers...
"Be gone!" sounded the creepy voices. "I've warned you!"
The trick-or-treaters were petrified.
"Woah! What're you doing here?" asked a familiar voice. "Didn't you know? It's haunted!"
"What? If we'd have known, we wouldn't have come in the first place!" answered the trick-or-treaters,
They ran home as fast as they could and told their parents but of course, adults don't believe in ghosts.
"Don't be silly!" they replied.

Maisey Gardner (10)
Even Swindon Primary School, Raybrook Park

THE WONDER OF SAFETY

An ear-splitting noise filled the air and Theo and Helena walked about, quaking with fear. Their lips were dry and as much as they hated this, these two young ones still fought through the spookiness of the corridor. Zombies appeared out of nowhere, trekking them down as spiders kept webs that spelt out words like 'blood' or 'you're done!'.
Screams were put in action from Helena as she stepped on a revolting trap that catapulted germ-spreading trash all around her!
After adding a pong so strong that almost everything fell from its place. Finally, a door opened up. Safety...

Alicia Atswei Adjei (10)
Even Swindon Primary School, Raybrook Park

24 BURROW STREET

Crunch! As I moved forward, I found something unusual. I started to lean forward to see. A mysterious, crumpled, damp sheet was lying in an abandoned street. It said on the sheet: '24, Burrow Street, I will meet you th-'
All of a sudden, the whole street went black. The lamp post had gone out! I looked around me but everything was black except a little house which stood on the edge of... Burrow Street.
Bung! Midnight had struck. A sudden chill shot down my spine...
"Meet me there!" echoed a voice.
"Arghh!" I stood there in fear.

Taishi Fu (9)
Even Swindon Primary School, Raybrook Park

HALLOWEEN SURPRISE!

Once upon a time, there lived a girl called Millie. She had ginger hair, brown eyes and was dressed as a witch for Halloween. Her mom and dad were calling her from downstairs, "Come, sweetie, we're going trick or treating." Millie replied, "Coming!"

So off they went.

When they came back, Millie heard weird noises like people talking and clapping in her wardrobe so she hid under the bed. The doors of the wardrobe opened. She peeked who it was and it was her grandma and Millie's friend, Daisy. Her nana and friend were laughing but Millie was scared.

Paula Szumska (10)
Even Swindon Primary School, Raybrook Park

THE FOREST OF WHISPERING TREES

In the dark and spooky Spooksville, where only monsters lurk and the moon was always full, lived a grotesque zombie-boy.
On the other side of the forest of whispering trees lived a small boy named Jack.
One evening, Jack decided to enter the spooky forest. Soon the zombie-boy realised that someone was in the forest and Jack realised he was being watched. The problem for Jack was that every time he hid behind a tree, it whispered to the zombie-boy where he was.
Suddenly, from out of a rustling bush sprang the zombie-boy.
"Gotcha!" and Jack became a zombie-boy.

Emily Karina Buckley-Wells (7)
Even Swindon Primary School, Raybrook Park

SHHH! DON'T TURN BACK

Once upon a time, there was a girl named Daisy. She was very scared of ghosts!
One day, Daisy decided to find out if ghosts existed so she decided to go into a haunted castle. Daisy was very scared and terrified. When she opened the door, the bats came flying towards her! Daisy screamed with fear. Suddenly, a voice whispered. "Why have you come here?"
Daisy saw tables moving around in the house, lights going on and off, bloody footprints, blood on walls. Suddenly, someone touched her from the back. Daisy turned around and saw a headless man! Daisy fainted...

Anora D'souza (9)
Even Swindon Primary School, Raybrook Park

AMONG US

An ear-piercing noise could be heard outside Chloe's bedroom, she got into her pyjamas. Sirens could be heard and when they got further away, only silence could be heard. She thought nothing of it and turned on her black radio to hear that an escaped prisoner had been sighted around her area. Chloe quickly turned it off and got into bed. Creaking and other strange noises were heard from the bedroom but Chloe took no notice and began to go to sleep. She then heard someone come up the stairs and she panicked.
She then heard something.
"Got you!"

Ellie-Maie Green (10)
Even Swindon Primary School, Raybrook Park

BOB THE FRIENDLY GHOST

Once in a haunted house, there was a ghost called Bob. He was friendly.
"Where am I?" questioned Bob.
The next day, he went adventuring and he found two other ghosts, Tallina and Connor. Both of them had paper to make a plan. While they were making an amazing plan, they found a barricaded door and because they were ghosts, all of them thought, *we could just go through the door!* They went through the door and experienced the outdoors and fresh air. That's the story of how Bob, Tallina and Connor escaped the dark, haunted house...

Alicja Trzeciak (9)
Even Swindon Primary School, Raybrook Park

TURNING TIME

One morning, a teacher called Zack thought that it would be a normal day of teaching but then the time was turned...
Ten seconds later, the school was gone and it was a combat zone. The guns shot until Zack noticed that the enemies were zombies! Zack wondered if he was dreaming, but unfortunately for him, he wasn't. Luckily, it was only him in the smallest trench. He suddenly realised that everybody from his class were the enemies. He named them all. Nathalia, Lillie, Sophie and Mia.
A few shots later, the school was back but his students were missing...

Evie Adams (10)
Even Swindon Primary School, Raybrook Park

MIST MAN

On a full moon, Lucy was going trick or treating with her friends. Mist was everywhere! She turned around and her friends were gone. All she could see was a man walking towards her. Lucy ran and ran as fast as she could until she was in an eerie forest. The girl looked around and continued running when she saw the man getting closer. The mist was spreading but she saw an abandoned house. Lucy went inside and everything froze.
"Hello," Lucy whispered.
She heard a drop. Was it blood or water? She felt teeth. *Bam!* Game over for Lucy.

Miriam Diakite (11)
Even Swindon Primary School, Raybrook Park

HOUSE OF SLIME

I've seen this house every day on the way home from school. Today is the day I pluck up the courage to enter. Feeling the fear running through my body from my head to my toes, I creep through...
"Yuck!"
The smell is disgusting, it burns my nose. I tiptoe towards the stairs but suddenly freeze. There, right in front of me, I see it. It's alive! It's green, it's moving. I can see the bubbles of this deadly slime. I turn and run, faster than I've ever run before, like Sonic. I fall to the floor... I'm safe now.

Jaydon Warren Wright (8)
Even Swindon Primary School, Raybrook Park

HORROR IN THE HOSPITAL

Izzy tripped over and hurt her ankle. She needed to go to the hospital. The nurses were breathing heavily like monsters, how strange! Izzy had to go for an X-ray in a wheelchair.
On the way, she saw a nurse turning into a green monster! Izzy and her mum panicked and hid in the medicine room. They tried to find some medicine for the monster nurse.
Then the monster nurse found them, Izzy distracted the monster nurse with a silly little dance in the wheelchair. Mum found the medicine but smashed it on the floor. Mum started to turn green.

Isabelle Lola Giles (8)
Even Swindon Primary School, Raybrook Park

THE MISLED TRICK-OR-TREATER

One Halloween night on October 31st, a young boy thought he would go on a normal trick or treating experience but little did he know that the terror had just begun. About halfway into the night, young Joe smelt the stench of his dead uncle, Barry. Due to Joe's sense of curiosity, he followed the mysterious smell. It led to an abandoned house which was covered in cobwebs and a photo of Queen Lacey with moving eyes.
Then Joe saw his uncle and he said, mysteriously, "I have been waiting for you!" Then only blood was seen...

Amelia Husband (10)
Even Swindon Primary School, Raybrook Park

BEWARE OF THE BALLOON

One day, some boys went to an abandoned theme park. It was 12.31pm and once they got through the gates it turned pitch-black. They could not see for ten minutes. Suddenly, a light. They followed it to a balloon. It was white and red with blue and green spots. They heard a bang from behind. They looked behind. Nothing was there. They looked back, the balloon was gone but there was something written in red paint, no, blood! 'Beware'. The balloon appeared again. One boy reached for the balloon and he was gone quick as a lightning bolt.

Jennifer Tregunna (8)
Even Swindon Primary School, Raybrook Park

THE LAST DAY?

One day, Mia went outside when it was sunny. She played with her kite near a creepy tree.

"Oh no!" she said.

Her kite got stuck inside the tree! Then she went home crying.

The next day, she needed to stay in her terrifying house because of thunder and lightning. Mia was sat at her desk doing her homework. Then she heard whispering voices coming from the window. She went to it and saw a figure in the darkness and every time lightning struck, you could hear terrifying, creepy screams and you could see... a clown!

Aleksandra Ola Krason (11)
Even Swindon Primary School, Raybrook Park

THE VAMPIRE

Once upon a time, there was a deadly vampire. He owned a haunted house. One night it was Halloween. He didn't like when people knocked on his door so he had an idea. It was every time someone knocked on his door, he would grab them and suck their blood!
Anyway, he only liked children's blood so that's what he did and two years later he stopped because he didn't feel like it was the best thing. Then the next year, it was Halloween. Children went but instead of grabbing them, he gave delicious sweets!

Bruna Rangel (9)
Even Swindon Primary School, Raybrook Park

DEADLY DETENTION

One rainy and horrific night, there were four stupid kids who went to an abandoned school. Some of the people heard whispering voices and figures in the darkness. When the children went near the hallway, they heard a child singing but when they went near the singing, it stopped. The child ran towards one of the kids and ate them alive!
One hour later, they saw a girl and asked her if she knew the way out but then she turned around and they saw that she had no eyes and her lips were sewn together.

Noemi Kufera (9)
Even Swindon Primary School, Raybrook Park

CHINA DOLL

Alicia was walking in the forest. She came across an abandoned shack. Intrigued, Alicia wandered over to it, the windows were boarded up. Suddenly, the rickety door swung open. Reluctantly, Alicia stepped inside. The inside looked ordinary but dusty. On the shelf was a china doll.
"Creepy!" Alicia muttered.
A flash of lightning, the china doll was gone. Another flash of lightning, she reappeared, holding a knife. Alicia's blood-curdling shriek shattered the silence...

Eden Grace Giles (11)
Even Swindon Primary School, Raybrook Park

THE SCHOOL TRIP

One day there was a school and they went on a school trip to Deanfield. They played lots of football.
When they went to bed, they heard a weird sound coming from the attic but they left it.
The next day they went up to the attic and saw a lot of skulls and eyeballs. They ran back upstairs and told a teacher.
The teacher said, "Okay!" then the teacher went down there and got eaten so the kids went down there and they were never to be seen again...

Tom Woolford (9)

Even Swindon Primary School, Raybrook Park

A GRAVEYARD SURPRISE

I'm walking to lunch. A spine-tingling scream echoes from the graveyard.
"Hello?" I cautiously ask.
"I'm here!" someone replies mistily.
In front of me, I see blood. Nearly having a heart attack, I follow the trail. Something cold and muddy taps me. I jump back and let out a screech. Butterflies fill me and I run behind a rock. Sweat patches cover me!
I look back, another. I blink, an army.
Thousands of ghostly zombies surround me. I can't breathe. Unexpectedly, I am attacked.
I am no more. Instead, a deadly creature roaming freely through the dark, cold winter street.

Jaina Ellen Sarr (9)
Frome Vale Academy, Downend

THE NIGHTMARE

Darkness arrived as I crept through the town, I couldn't see a thing. Unexpectedly, I heard a scream. I could only see a bloody path on the road so I decided to follow it...
It took me to a gloomy torch so I used it. Once again, the scream. I went towards it. All of a sudden, the scream came again and again. I wanted to shout but nothing came out. I followed the noise until I found... a house. There were ghosts guarding the house. I crept in slowly. A vampire came towards me.
Wait... it was a dream!

Fatima Munir (8)
Frome Vale Academy, Downend

THE SPOOKY TALE OF THE GRIFFIN

A boy went to the woods when all of a sudden, a griffin came and took him! The parents of the boy were upset and decided to get him back. They found the griffin and a space ship. Quickly, they jumped in and went towards the griffin. As quick as a flash, the parents got into the griffin's roost. They saw their son! Slowly, they crept towards their son...
"Grrr!"
The griffin appeared and fell. They took their son and ran away. The griffin chased after them but they got back home.

Wyatt Tristan Smith (8)
Frome Vale Academy, Downend

A MURDERER

The clock struck at twelve o'clock. My hair was flying in the wind. I jumped out of bed and stepped in blood. I ran downstairs and saw a knife. At that moment, I knew it was a murderer. I chased but it was too fast and hid. I ran upstairs and the floor was shaking. I saw a knife on the floor. I ran to it before the murderer could get it again. After he dropped it, I grabbed it. He ran even faster away. Suddenly, he ran towards the back garden. He climbed the fence and he ran away!

Endri Ahmeti (8)
Frome Vale Academy, Downend

THE TERRIFIED SISTERS

One night, me and my sister were in the caravan and we heard a thump... We looked out the window and saw a terrifying killer clown! Me and my sister ran out of the caravan to try and fight it. We could not do it so we went to tell Mum and Grandad. We ran to get in the caravan but it chased me so I locked the door. I was so scared! I found out it was just my dad dressed up!
"Dad! You scared us so much!"

Lily Millmore (7)
Godshill Primary School, Godshill

THE HALLOWEEN NIGHTMARE

I finally opened the door. I still couldn't see anything. Although the bloodstains had grown darker, hardened almost. Was there really anyone here or was I just imagining... again? I was going trick or treating, haunted or not. Nothing was going to spoil my night!
Moments later, I was lifting my hand to knock but before I could touch the door, I was pulled inside...
A voice said, "Say nothing, tell nobody of this, what's about to happen will stay secret forever!"
I screamed for help, nothing came out. I tried again. Nothing, as if I'd lost my voice...

Daisy Print (10)
Grange Junior School, Stratton St Margaret

THE HALLOWEEN FRIGHT!

It was Halloween night, all was quiet. It was a fun night for most, however, not for these three lonesome trick-or-treaters.
They were approaching their final house and were getting chills all over. They rang the doorbell and waited... Suddenly, the door flew open by itself. Their curiosity swallowed their fear, so they entered.
The house was creepy, abandoned and cobwebbed from corner to corner. They ascended the old, creaky steps leading to a small room with a wardrobe that they played hide-and-seek in until they realised they had company. They were never heard from again...

Samuel Roach (10)
Grange Junior School, Stratton St Margaret

UNDER THE BED

Peering out from under my adorned duvet, darkness spread over my room like a blanket. Was I alone? Reading the darkness like a witch, I could spot my chalky, saturated wardrobe crying in a corner, wishing it was somewhere else. Twitching behind it, there lurked a far worse situation - spiders! It was an infestation! Creeping out from under the bed, a dim, lifeless silhouette approached. Elbows like daggers, arms as hairy as a yeti. It advanced. Following my natural instinct, I called for help. I waited and waited. There was no reply. Fearing death, giving in, I walked towards it...

Carly Macmillan (10)
Grange Junior School, Stratton St Margaret

WHAT GOES AROUND COMES AROUND

A power cut sent the house into darkness. He continued to amble down the arthritic stairs to examine his recent kill. The door closed. Whilst dissecting his latest victim, a sinister figure emerged from the shadows and started to edge towards him. Turning to run, he reached for the door but its handle was as sharp as a machete.

Suddenly, an agonising pain erupted in his left shoulder, dismembering his entire arm. A similar pain jabbed into his right leg, severing it. A blanket of gloom enclosed... the cold, musty odour left the room, dragging the murderous figure alongside it.

Kezia Ruby Palmer (10)
Grange Junior School, Stratton St Margaret

FALLING...

As I climbed the stairs to a dusty, abandoned attic leading to potential terror, I noticed that something inside me didn't feel right. My stomach was churning and my palms were sweating with fear. I finally reached the top of the staircase and I saw a shadowy, sinister figure creep into a broken wardrobe and vanish. Suddenly, I felt an icy chill trickle down the back of my spine. I started to walk towards the wardrobe.

As I opened the rusty door, my feelings started to slowly drain out of my soul as I fell, fell into a deep blackness.

Isabel Steele (10)

Grange Junior School, Stratton St Margaret

A LURKING FIGURE

Alone in a forest, it's pitch-black and the trees around me are casting long, ominous shadows. No Mum. No Dad. I'm stood here without a torch, fearing for my life. Suddenly, an eerie sound filters through the air. I blink. My eyes open to see a dark figure lingering in front of me. I run. My legs start to ache. He's catching up. My legs are too tired. I stop, exhausted... My last memory is of an evil face, bewitched and sinister, looking down at me and all that I could think about was death, *only* death...

Harry Myrtle (11)
Grange Junior School, Stratton St Margaret

THE DOLL

What was that? I could hear the screeching of nails being dragged along the floorboards. As I slowly crept up the stairs, I could see an unfamiliar shadow. Suddenly, the shadow twitched! It was a doll. A creepy, petrifying doll. I tried to scream but all I heard was a spooky silence. Then the figure slowly walked towards me. All of a sudden, the doll stopped and the lights flickered. As I stared at the creepy doll, I noticed another head lingering above me...
"Aghh!" I screamed.
"I got you!" said my mum.

Grace Hayward (10)
Grange Junior School, Stratton St Margaret

DARK DREAM

As daylight faded, the moon rose and the fog descended like a blanket over the city. Lying unconscious, I was trapped in a claustrophobic room, away from the outsiders. There was no escaping. As my heartbeat was rising, a musty odour filled my lungs, awakening me. Where was I? My eyes flickered, someone was with me. A black figure emerged before my eyes. Trembling with fear, I stared into a pair of piercing eyes.
The ghostly shadow spoke, "I have been waiting for you!"
My mind was racing, was this a dream?

Javeah Simpson (11)
Grange Junior School, Stratton St Margaret

THE BASEMENT

It enveloped the room. Darkness. My bloodshot eyes burst open, I was blind. I could see nothing. I could hear noises, eerie noises. There was light. I was in a basement. A sign said: *Once You Come Here, You Can Never Go Back.* I froze. I felt a pin insert into my ice-cold neck. I tried to scream but nothing came out. I fell to the ground. Ghosts, vampires and zombies appeared everywhere, looming over me. I wished it was just a dream. I hoped it was just a dream, was I dead? Was this the end of me?

Paige Roberts (11)
Grange Junior School, Stratton St Margaret

ALONE

As I awake in the darkness of light, twigs snap and my heart pounds like a beating drum. I am covered in mud and my clothes are wrecked. What am I doing here? I don't remember anything. I've started to panic. I am all alone at dawn without a light or a phone. I walk forward, a door creaks open. I'm in.
The walls whisper but then I realise I'm in an old, abandoned asylum for the undead. I trip over a torch, it works! Blood-covered stairs roam before my eyes. A hand crawls in front of me...

Lucia Johnston (10)
Grange Junior School, Stratton St Margaret

KNOCK, KNOCK, KNOCK!

"Why are the lights on?" Bella wondered, walking towards the school.
She reached up and knocked on the rickety, old door. There was only silence, so she knocked again. *Knock! Knock!* At that moment, as she was walking away, the door creaked open slightly. Bella cautiously tiptoed back to the door and whispered, "Trick or treat!"
She slowly lifted her sweet-filled bucket and waited... Just then, a lumpy, grotesque, horrible hand shot out and dropped a creepy, chocolate egg into her bucket. Bella ran away screaming and the door slowly closed with a creak and a witch's cackle!

Beatrice Brazier (8)
Harewood Junior School, Tuffley

THE WITCH AND THE DITCH

There was a boy called John. His mum shouted,
"John! Don't go in the ditch!"
He didn't listen and he went into the ditch and it got foggy.
He heard a creepy voice saying, "John? John?"
He got nervous! He got grabbed by the leg!
"Help!" screamed John, scratching his nails on the soil. He tried to get out but he couldn't.
Then there was silence.

The next day, all the people were wondering why there were marks on the grass...

Sam Jackman (8)
Hawkesbury CE Primary School, Hawkesbury Upton

THE MURDER

Lyla and Maya had just got back from a walk in the woods. They ran to their bedrooms and there was something awful on their beds - blood! Suddenly, there was a horrific scream from the girls.
"Arghh! A knife!"
The next night, Lyla and Maya met up outside to investigate the murder. Just then, they saw a trail of blood. They followed it...
A few hours later, they got to a cabin. It was the one from the woods. It was the witch's husband! The two friends nervously walked in...
"Maya!"
Maya was gone. Would she ever return?

Maddi Evie Just (9)
Heamoor Community Primary School, Heamoor

MY WALK TO SCHOOL!

I am walking to school when I hear something. Screams. I look through the school's window but it's splattered with blood. I turn to run away and hear cackling but don't stop running. Then it becomes too much and I have to turn around, but I can't. I look down and notice the edge of a knife... I fall to my knees but I can't feel anything. I turn around to see the clown about to speak.
"Do you want to see a magic trick?" asks the clown, but it is too late, I am dead and everything is gone.

Jowan Thomson (10)
Heamoor Community Primary School, Heamoor

THE DOLL WHO LIVED!

One day, I woke up and I was in an attic. I looked around to notice I was alone!

"I wonder why I'm here," I wondered.

Suddenly, I heard a scream and a crash. Before I knew it, I saw a doll with blood on her face. I screamed but nothing came out. Now I was really getting worried! The doll looked at me and grabbed me. I closed my eyes so tight, I thought I was going to die. All of a sudden, the grip came loose.

Then I heard, "Tricked ya!"

It was my mum, cackling.

Ellysia Russell (9)
Heamoor Community Primary School, Heamoor

THE HAUNTED HOUSE

One rainy day, Maya and her friends were walking in the woods. They came across an abandoned house. They decided to take a look. Maya was the first to start noticing things that weren't normal. They all went upstairs to take a look. The stairs were creaky and old. Then they saw something in the corner of the room. They ran for it, dashed out the house and made it out but something was chasing them. While running through the woods, they escaped but Maya ended up with some strange marks on her body.

Ashleigh Rose Nicholas (9)
Heamoor Community Primary School, Heamoor

THE HAUNTED HOUSE OF SIR BONGLE!

As the petrified trick-or-treaters stepped onto Sir Charles Bongle's doorstep, Bill reached out his quivering right hand. The door was encrusted in silver and overgrown ivy. Bill knocked rapidly as his hand was shaking so much. He managed to do it but there was no one there so Terry pushed the door open. *Creak!* The door swung open like someone was pulling it for them. The two twins crept down the hallway. The paintings looked like they were staring at them and they were! Terry and Bill started to run down the hallway in a panic...

Joseph Thompson-Gibbs (9)
Horsley CE Primary School, Horsley

CREATURE OF THE LONG-LOST LAGOON

Running through the depths of the forest, Olive dragged her frightened cousin, Poppy, to the ancient swamp that nobody visited anymore.
"Olive... are you sure this is safe?" Poppy asked with a stutter in her voice.
Olive nodded with an excited smile.

Once they reached the swamp, Olive noticed something in the water and nudged her frozen cousin.
Poppy looked at Olive, then looked at the water and turned on her flashlight, but *whoosh!* Poppy was being dragged into the water by this unknown creature!
"Poppy!" Olive screamed, holding onto her drowning cousin helplessly as Poppy slowly stopped.
She disappeared.

Shaakirah Miah (9)
Nailsworth CE Primary School, Nailsworth

THE DARING CHILDREN

Wandering around, three children headed for the deserted forest. A cold wind shivered down their spines. A shadow appeared, there right in front of them was a stomach-churning, fur-covered werewolf. It began to howl.
Moments fled by, the children stood there like statues. Thoughts rushed through their heads. *What to do? Where to go?* As the werewolf crept forwards, a putrid smell filled their nostrils. The moon shone bright in the inky, black sky. As the werewolf pounced forwards, a flash of electrifying lightning filled the sky. Ghosts fluttered around. Where had the three daring children vanished to?

Jessica Benjamin (11)
Nailsworth CE Primary School, Nailsworth

THE MYSTERIOUS CAPTURE

"Woah, this looks very t-terrifying! Where am I?" questioned Tilly as she looked at the walls in disgust.
Oh, wait, I think I remember now, but it doesn't make sense, thought Tilly.
It all started when she slowly walked up to this grotesque house, thinking it was just scary because of Halloween. When Tilly walked up, the door opened and she got pulled inside!
Now she was there in a creepy, moonlit house. All of the paint was coming off the walls and it had spiderwebs everywhere.
"Wait, you don't think it could be a ghost?"

Lexie Hankins (10)
Nailsworth CE Primary School, Nailsworth

THE SPOOKY ABANDONED PLACE

I finally came to the last house. It looked really abandoned and it didn't look like people lived there. I knocked on the door but no one answered. I was just about to leave but someone answered but it wasn't a normal person, it was a ghost!
I said, "Trick or treat!"
The ghost disappeared and a vampire came with some treats and said, "Take one!"
I took one, ate it and I was poisoned!
I yelled at the vampire, "Why were you trying to poison me?"
I started to walk through the park but I was getting followed...

Lucy Sian Hope Thomas (11)
Nailsworth CE Primary School, Nailsworth

FOREST OF NIGHTMARES

It was an ordinary Wednesday night and Charlie Smith was getting ready for bed. Cautiously, he crept into bed, pulling his blankets up to his nose. Slowly, Charlie's eyes began to close and he drifted off to sleep. Charlie woke up suddenly and felt some rustling under his bed. Next, he found himself leaning over the side of the bed, only to find long, prickly roots crawling out. Then he noticed the bush growing out of his drawers. Soon, his whole room was a dark forest! "Arghh!" he tried to scream but thick, green leaves muffled his words.

Matilda Hope Mechan (10)
Nailsworth CE Primary School, Nailsworth

FREEDOM AT LAST!

Here I am, petrified, hiding behind a crate in the bedroom of a creepy, abandoned house, watching my captor search for me. Then something catches my eye. The keys hanging off his belt. I dart out from behind the crate and run out of the room. The man behind the mask chases me but he slips down the stairs, knocking himself out cold. I grab the keys off his belt and one by one, try them in the four padlocks.

Crack! One down, three to go...

Soon, I have the next two unlocked.

Crack! Finally, the last one gone! *Freedom!*

Evan Manders-Trett (9)

Nailsworth CE Primary School, Nailsworth

HALLOWEEN HORROR

It was the 31st October, I was dressed as a spooky, scary skeleton and I was delighted with how much candy I'd gathered! There was only one house to go to - Tooke Road, number sixty-three.
I knocked on the door and said, "Trick or treat!"
As I did so, the door swung open but there was nobody there. As I walked in, I saw a French guillotine with blood dripping from the blade. As I looked around, I saw a bucket full of heads. I screamed and ran out. As I turned the corner, I saw a shadowy figure...

Callum Miles (10)
Nailsworth CE Primary School, Nailsworth

A FORBIDDEN BOOK OF SPELLS

Once there was a boy called Harry. He was eight years old. Harry's dad is a ghost hunter and one day, Harry followed his dad to work. He found himself outside a big, old house. He went through two doors and entered a big hallway which echoed. There was a door left open and Harry walked towards it. He saw lots of books, one caught Harry's eye so he opened it. It was a book of spells. Harry read out a poem and instantly got sucked into the book...
"Oh no!"
What would happen to Harry...?

Cameron Michael Keith Gardiner (8)
Nailsworth CE Primary School, Nailsworth

THE GREEN EYES

We knew we should not go into the house. Our mum said it was haunted but we wanted to see a ghost!
It was cold, dark and creepy. We heard the floor creaking. We turned around and saw something move.
My brother screamed, "Ghost!" and ran out of the house.
I said, "Come back!"
He did not listen. I felt something on my leg. I looked down, all I could see were green eyes.
The ghost turned out to be a black cat who was just as scared as we were! I took her to meet him.

Cameron Lord (9)
Nailsworth CE Primary School, Nailsworth

TRICK OR TREAT, OR IS IT?

A chilly, cold night and I was dressed, ready, treat bucket in hand.

"Trick or treat!" I cried.

I passed the last house, there was a lane. I wondered if there were more houses. I came across a woodland, it felt creepy and silent. I saw a figure in the dark. It moved so fast then appeared in front of me. I was terrified! I was stuck, I couldn't move! Fear gripped me.

"You're a vampire!" I cried out loud.

I dropped my bucket and ran. The boy picked up my bucket.

"This costume's great!"

He filled up his bag.

Georgia Lynne McCarthy (11)
Padstow Primary School, Padstow

ONE DISMAL NIGHT

It was a dark, dismal night. The crows had just gone to bed and the bats had just awoken. It struck midnight and it started to rain. It was so cold, I couldn't feel my fingertips. My toes were cold, my hair was frozen and I couldn't feel anything except the cold rush brushing through my hair. In the distance, I started to see a tall figure.
"Hello?" I whispered. "Who's there?"
In slow motion, I crept towards it and all of a sudden, the person shouted, "Found you!"
Of course, it was my brother, scaring me!

Lizzie Wickins (9)
Padstow Primary School, Padstow

MOVING PICTURES

One bitter cold night, Cara heard something moving upstairs but thought nothing of it.
The next morning, she went into the attic to see what made the spine-chilling noise and she was shocked, everything had moved!
Everything scattered on the floors. She was petrified.
For the next three days, she didn't dare to step foot in the attic. She didn't know what to do, she didn't know who to tell. She kept on telling herself it was the wind. She brought herself to tell her mum or dad and her dad turned to her and she helped clean up.

Olivia Griffiths (9)
Padstow Primary School, Padstow

HAUNTED PEANUT BUTTER IN A JAR!

A long, long time ago, a boy called Johnny went to explore an abandoned house.
After hours of exploring, Johnny found a dusty, ancient-looking jar of peanut butter and made the biggest mistake of his life... He opened the jar of peanut butter. After that, things just got worse.
First, the peanut butter exploded all over his face, then a ghost spat goo on his head, then the lights started flickering. That was just his brother. Oh no, his mischievous brother!
After what felt like hours, but it was just five minutes, Johnny ran home to bed.

Finley Bray (10)
Padstow Primary School, Padstow

THE DAY OF THE DEAD

Four years ago, someone called Kai fell off a boat.
An hour later, his friends found him on the beach and took him to the hospital, but that hospital was not the kind that worked on people!
They went into the hospital and found the doctor inside. They put him on the table.
The doctor said, "I'm not very good on people but I will try!"
He got a strange collar out of a drawer and put it on Kai. Then he got a big needle, squirted the antivenom into his body and turned him into a zombie!

Harry Symons (8)
Padstow Primary School, Padstow

THE VAMPIRE UNDER MY BED

At night, it was dark and I was asleep. I felt something under my bed. It was spooky! I wanted to scream but I couldn't because I was scared to scream. It was difficult for me, but when I looked under there, I couldn't see anything. Today was really scary!
When I woke up, I looked under my bed and saw a green, slimy monster with red, blood-shot eyes staring at me. I screamed so loud, I even worried myself. I kept dreaming that the monster was going to eat me. It was just a dream!

Faith Chown (5)
Padstow Primary School, Padstow

MONSTER IN THE HOUSE

Long, long ago, in a haunted house, was a haunted cupboard with ghosts and a vampire in the house. A trick-or-treater knocked at the door.

"Arghh!" said the trick-or-treater, but she did not know the vampire was her mum!

Her mum did not know something was moving behind her, it was a zombie! It was scary! She was frightened and her mum was too. They did not know the zombie was the girl's dad! They ran to their haunted house to hide under the bed until morning came.

Ella Hoskin (6)

Padstow Primary School, Padstow

THE BLACK DEATH

One gloomy night, the trees whirled and looked like hands coming out to kill you. A man was trekking through the woods that day from nowhere, a giant, hairy rat jumped out from a dark, green bush and sank his rotten, yellow teeth into his leg. He let out a wail!
The next day, he, or should I say it, felt something touching its leg. It threw the covers off to reveal a pink, hairy rat's tail! It jumped out of bed and two big teeth grew and lots of hair...

Joey Flide (11)
Padstow Primary School, Padstow

JACK THE SKELETON

Once upon a time, there was a skeleton called Jack. He was a boy first but now he was a skeleton.
One day when Jack was a little boy, he walked down a spooky road where the haunted house stood. Two ghosts lived there. They got murdered in the house. Jack looked into a magic mirror. He saw he was a skeleton! He made friends with the ghosts.
"There's no place like bones!"

Heath Noon (7)
Padstow Primary School, Padstow

THE MONSTER UNDER THE BED!

One monstrous night, there was a girl called Alisha. There was a storm and she was scared! Alisha was not brave at all, she was scared of everything. She was with her dad. It seemed that she was going out.
The banshee came into the bedroom and hid under the beautifully terrifying four-legged bed with fake blood on it. Alisha came back and saw a figure, it was a creepy person! The banshee popped out and she screamed.
Her dad came in and killed the banshee and they lived perfectly fine in their house which they loved.

Shaylene Leigh (8)
Perry Court E-ACT Academy, Hengrove

THE DEAD OF NIGHT

It was getting dark, there was one more thing I had to do. I had to get the treats before the children came, but where from? The shops were all shut because of a fire.

The doorbell rang, I jumped to my feet with the fear of not having any treats. I opened the door but to my surprise, there was nothing there other than an odd-looking box. I grabbed the box and took it inside. For a moment, I stared at the box but then I decided to open it. Inside was a note saying: 'I've found you!'

Lilly Joan Leona Woodward (10)
Perry Court E-ACT Academy, Hengrove

THE MYSTERIOUS CAKE

It was a dark and gloomy night and Leo went to his friend's house. He was told that he could have a yummy cake so as you'd probably expect, he ate it. Then he went to the toilet. Surprisingly, Leo became an evil panther! He bashed through the door and started ripping the sofas. Leo started to pounce and leap down the street. Out of the corner of his beady eye, he saw *humans!* With that, Leo started to eat them! Sadly and horrifyingly, the poor, innocent and sweet people were murdered.

Violet Walker (9)
Perry Court E-ACT Academy, Hengrove

ONE CHILLING NIGHT

It all started on the night of Halloween, it was dark and very windy outside. I was sat watching my favourite TV programme when I heard a noise behind me which made me jump. I turned around and saw a shadow move across the window. I ran to my bedroom, petrified and hid under my bed.
While under the bed, I heard a tapping on the window.
After a while of continuing, I had to have a look and all it was was a tree branch banging on the window in the wind!

Tia Rebecca Hayfield (9)
Perry Court E-ACT Academy, Hengrove

SPOOKY

Once upon a spooky time, there was a creepy figure called Slappy. He had terrifying friends and he had a plan to terrorise a city.
The first house he knocked on was a librarian called Mr Mortian. He crept in and ran past him so he turned Mr Mortian into a monster! He was a green monster!
In the second house he knocked on was a boy called Drake. He got turned into a monster too so Slappy went back home with them and they slept.

Mason Jones (9)
Perry Court E-ACT Academy, Hengrove

NIGHTS OF THE SPOOKS

One day, a new girl moved into the haunted house. Everyone told her she'd moved into a haunted house. She had moved into the wrong house! She didn't know what everyone meant so she went into the attic.
She got in there and saw a vampire and screamed. It was her dad!
He shouted, "I am a vampire!" He turned around and said, "Do you think this is cool? I am getting ready for Halloween but where were you?"

Grace Jeffries (10)
Perry Court E-ACT Academy, Hengrove

DISAPPEARING ROAD

We were walking home from a party.
One of my friends, Mia, exclaimed, "Let's take the shortcut through Disappearing Road!"
"No, people disappear there, remember Sarah and Jane?" I shouted.
"That's just an old story!" Maria screeched.
I was outvoted. As we walked, we could hear three footsteps. Then only two footsteps.
"Mia!" we shouted, yet no answer.
My stomach felt sick. Then there was only one pair of footsteps - mine. I could see the end. I ran...
"God, please let me get to the end, I'm gonna make it, please, I'm not gonna disap-"

Mya Wharton (10)
St Andrew's CE Junior School, Burnham-On-Sea

BUDDY THE ELF GONE BAD

Atticus didn't believe in elves. That Christmas, he got up and spotted an elf with the name tag 'Buddy'. He didn't remember owning an elf and definitely didn't believe in them so he ignored it. As he opened his presents, he saw Buddy.
"I didn't bring you downstairs!"
And although he ignored Buddy, he felt nervous. As Atticus pulled back the shower curtain, he saw Buddy again surrounded by the presents. He screamed and had an evil grin and his head turned all the way around.
"You haven't been very good this year!" Buddy chuckled. "I will haunt you!"

Dexter Pashley (9)
St Andrew's CE Junior School, Burnham-On-Sea

MYSTERIOUS WOODS

Jeff and Kevin had heard about the mysterious No Return Woods. People had said if you go in, you don't come out. Jeff and Kevin didn't believe them. After dark that day, they decided to go and investigate the mysterious woods. They took their torches and off they went. Jeff and Kevin entered the mysterious wood, tiptoeing through the crunchy leaves. They were scared!
All of a sudden, they reached a big, round empty space. They stepped forwards carefully and then *boom!*
Suddenly, the ground opened up underneath them and they never came out of the mysterious woods.

Tyler Mitchell (9)
St Andrew's CE Junior School, Burnham-On-Sea

THE MONSTER'S TEA

Ella was going to bed, worrying that a monster would eat her. Looking all around, she froze. She heard scratching on the floor and then the door. She didn't dare look under her bed but then she saw something behind her door.
It said, "Hello..."
"Hi... who are you?"
"I've been waiting for my tea under your bed!"
"What are you having?"
"You!"
"But... why me?"
"Because you're scared of me and you look very scrumptious, so if you don't mind, I'll eat you now!"

Keira Herniman (11)
St Andrew's CE Junior School, Burnham-On-Sea

THE ELF ON THE SHELF

Last year, I had an Elf on the Shelf called
Buddy, he was actually very good.
This year, I had a note that said 'I'm Buddy's
evil brother, find me'. This was no ordinary elf,
he was called Chucky. On the first night, he ate
chocolate number four from my calendar
before I could get to it.
The second night, he painted Pete with glittery
blue nail polish.
The third night, I saw him in the Christmas tree.
He had a tiny key and a note that said: 'Look in
the kitchen!'
There was a little elf door...
"Argh!"

April Lees (9)
St Andrew's CE Junior School, Burnham-On-Sea

MY TENSION

All of a sudden, his life changed. He stood in only pain and broken bits of his heart. Why did this start?
One dark, dangerous night, Tom Green stood in his basement. In the blink of an eye, the light started to flicker. He could see a gloomy, black, bold shadow.
A moment later, he heard a voice...
The voice spoke, "Show yourself now!"
Tom, who stood there in terror, took one step into the light. It was the horrible head teacher! Did she want revenge on him? Amazingly, she turned into a dragon and of course, she bit him...

Holly Pike (9)
St Andrew's CE Junior School, Burnham-On-Sea

ZOMBIE ATTACK

Once upon a time, there was a boy called Danny. He had a teddy named Bonnie.
One night, Bonnie came to life! Bonnie went on Danny's computer and played 'Zombies Attack'. She was fighting wave four when a zombie came up in front of the screen and reached out his slimy hand! He pulled Bonnie into the game!
Petrified, she ran away but some vampires caught her and gave her an infected bite. She turned into a vampire! She went out hunting with the others and caught lots of prey.
The next day, Danny woke and Bonnie was never found.

Isaac Burge (9)
St Andrew's CE Junior School, Burnham-On-Sea

ON HALLOWEEN NIGHT...

One Halloween, a girl called Millie walked out of her house and thought, *what a lovely night to go to Cackles Graveyard.* Millie saw something so she thought she would go and see. Suddenly... *bump!* Millie was falling down a deep hole. Millie was surprisingly crawling through pipes. Finally, she reached the end. There was a radio and it started talking.
It mumbled, "You are stuck in my house and will never get out!"
To this day, Millie is still in the house and trust me, you don't want to go there!

Leah Pike (9)
St Andrew's CE Junior School, Burnham-On-Sea

THE MYSTERIOUS MANSION

Bang! Something exploded in the distance. Tom sprinted forward and knew that he should look back. He came to a stop at a derelict mansion.
"Is it haunted?" Tom wondered as he saw a spider as big as a plump chicken crawling into a smashed window of the mansion.
After he saw that, he knew it must be haunted but he had no choice but to go in. As quiet as a mouse, Tom tiptoed into the haunted mansion. The door slammed shut behind him! Another door opened and out popped a black cat, but was it alive or dead?

Keira Snowball (10)
St Andrew's CE Junior School, Burnham-On-Sea

THE CREATURE IN THE CLOSET

Dear diary,
My parents left a few weeks ago, I've no idea what's happening. All I know is that there's something lurking in the shadows of my home and will only show itself when it knows that someone is truly alone and that it's okay to strike. I found this out yesterday as I heard whispering and it was saying something about how it's going to kill me. I also found a piece of writing in blood saying: 'I'll find you!'
I'm not sure how long it will take for it to find me...

Anumta Manzoor (11)
St Andrew's CE Junior School, Burnham-On-Sea

HOME ALONE

Today is Mum and Dad's wedding anniversary
so they went out and I'm home alone. I don't
think I am. No, really, I'm serious.
A few minutes ago, when I went to the toilet, I
walked in and found writing on the mirror. It
said: 'I will get you!' in blood. I went to the
downstairs toilet and a message was there too,
it said: 'You know you're next!'
I ran upstairs, avoiding as many things as I
could and locked myself in my room.
Wait, I think I saw something move...

Minahil Manzoor (9)
St Andrew's CE Junior School, Burnham-On-Sea

MYSTERY INTRUDER

It was an ordinary day, home alone, until I heard a bang. I ignored it and went to bed. Then I heard it again. I hid under my covers but slightly peeked out to keep an eye. All of a sudden, I heard footsteps along the creaky floor. I plucked up the courage to see what it was but there was no sign of anyone. I escaped and ran into the gloomy woods, then ran to my friend's house. I told her everything.
She said, "At least you are safe!"
I replied, "Yeah, but who was in my house?"

Sienna Bradshaw (11)
St Andrew's CE Junior School, Burnham-On-Sea

ATTIC OF HELL

As Max arrived at the old playground at 8am, he felt something brush past him. He turned but saw nothing but a shadow. He ran to his home but when he came home, all he saw was a red pool of blood. He ran to his room, tripped and fell into more blood!
Other rooms were locked, all but the attic. He walked up to it and heard intense breathing. He picked up a knife and searched for what was making this noise. It was a grey-haired toddler with piercing yellow eyes and sharp teeth immersed in blood...

Max Humphreys (10)
St Andrew's CE Junior School, Burnham-On-Sea

ARNOLD'S ADVENTURE

Legend has it there was once a man by the name of Arnold. He lived many years ago and one day, he went on an expedition in the hills of Alaska. He had set off, seeing the beautiful sights.

Then night came. He trekked for two miles and found an alcove in the side of a cliff face. He ventured in to discover it was a cave so once he'd got in, his torch revealed to him a bear - a *hungry* bear. A bear which was awake. He tried to run but it charged. Arnold was never seen again.

Michael Pettitt (11)
St Andrew's CE Junior School, Burnham-On-Sea

THE MONSTERS

One day there was this person who died by getting struck by lightning, falling wooden spikes and covered in lava. He turned into a zombie with both eyes hanging out but as soon as he moved, he turned to dust!
After a while, the dust blew around, then he turned into a detached skeleton. He started to scare people by separating his body.
Unfortunately, he got crushed by a brick.
A few days later, he became a ghost - a ghost that nobody could see.

Louie Reed (10)
St Andrew's CE Junior School, Burnham-On-Sea

UNRELIABLE...

Slithering strings of intestines spewing like exhaust fumes, skinless from flesh-eaters, boneless from bone-eaters. Nothing but a lifeless soul repossessed, starved, dazed, merciless, black holes in their eyes. Their irresistible grin screamed demonically. Thoughtless brains are swallowed from crippling depression. One shot can change a life. *Bang!* Mindless freaks, twitching, their exoskeleton unresponsive. What a child thought to be a world of cupcakes and rainbows turned out to be a world of unreliable, misshapen beasts. Like a flatline, the world was still ongoing. If only the world would stop to look for one moment... God has been forsaken.

Kiki Hayes (11)
Stratton Primary School, Stratton

BOB AND THE VOODOO DOLL

Bob had arrived, he was on an adventure! He could hear the distant howling of werewolves! Bob saw a slender man's face and the door opened. A bony white finger directing him forwards.

As he entered, the door slammed behind him, revealing the creepiest, most grotesque doll ever! She began to talk and walk towards him.

"Want to play hide-and-seek?" she croaked scarily.

Bob fled.

"No!" he yelled.

"Pappy!" the doll cried.

A killer clown grabbed him by the neck, threatening him. Bob could see the doll with a bloody, silver knife in hand. What would she do?

Niamh Collen (10)
Stratton Primary School, Stratton

THE UNUSUAL NIGHT

Once there was a cottage hidden in the woods. One night, the wind was howling and the leafless trees were tapping on the window like spiny fingers. The wolves were howling at the moon. The lights flickered. Spiderwebs like golden string were sitting in every corner of the dusty rooms. Suddenly, pictures started shaking and crashing to the ground. Looking around in a daze, sat an elderly man in a rocking chair. What was happening? The man hid under his chair, shaking in fright. Within seconds, all the lights went out and a dark shadow reached for the door handle...

Lily Glasby (8)
Stratton Primary School, Stratton

ELLIE'S NIGHTMARE

In the distance, you could see the gorgon rising from the cemetery of the castle over the sea. A small girl called Ellie witnessed this and was so curious, she ventured over to the path at low tide, over to the castle.
It was cold and deserted inside the castle. There were draughts flying from every direction. Ellie's blood turned cold. She turned around to catch a glimpse of a snake strand. Ellie closed her eyes and fought. It was no good, Medusa would turn her into stone if she turned! Ellie retreated. Suddenly, she woke. It was a nightmare!

Maebh Collen (8)
Stratton Primary School, Stratton

IN THE ZOMBIE WORLD!

In the heart of a haunted house lived a person called Lilly. She lived near the forest.
One night, she heard a bang on the window and saw zombies. She panicked, and when she turned around, there was a zombie! She screamed! There was blood everywhere, but no one knew what happened...
The next day on the news, there was a zombie peering. People locked everything and hid, but there was one person who stood up for everyone and went to the forest and killed the zombies.
One year later, he saved the day and zombies were extinct forever!

Lulu Hayes (8)
Stratton Primary School, Stratton

ONE SPOOKY NIGHT

One spooky night when the moon was full, a witch was zooming through the sky. A short distance away were three feral children called Thomas, Jamie and Fern were playing on their bikes.
When the witch landed, she invited the children with a cackle in her house and said, "If you come in, I'll let you have some sweets!"
When the children realised that the witch was a meanie and planned to eat them, they swiftly grabbed the witch's wand and quickly escaped. The children never, ever, ever went with a stranger again!

Amilia May Boundy (8)
Stratton Primary School, Stratton

DROWNING ON THE BEACH

Emma, who wanted to enjoy the sun, went to the beach. When she was at the beach, she found a cave and wanted to explore. She went inside and screamed when she saw an ugly sight. It was a witch! The witch began to stir something in the cauldron which looked lumpy and disgusting. Emma saw outside that the tide was drawing in closer and closer every second. Suddenly, the witch called Emma closer towards the sea...
"Oh no, I'm too late, I am blocked in!" Emma explained to the witch. What was she going to do?

Megan Price (10)
Stratton Primary School, Stratton

THE BOY WHO WAS EATEN BY GHOSTS

As he trotted to school, things didn't feel the same as they usually did. He walked in, scared for his life. He saw a flash of light, a bolt of terror ran down his spine. He tried to get out the door but it was locked. Suddenly, he turned around and there was a ghost as pale as chalk and as sly as a fox.
"Hello?" said the boy, trembling with fear.
"Don't worry, it's just me!"
He screamed. A bony, white hand grabbed him, pulling him into a room and locking the creaky door...

Thea Gregory (10)
Stratton Primary School, Stratton

MY BLOOD OR YOUR BLOOD

One foggy day, there was a girl called Luna. She loved cake and ate some. The cake was poisoned and Luna turned into a zombie. People were afraid of zombies. They fled to New York overnight. Luna was alone in the basement of her home. She found tiny drops of blood and by cutting her finger mixed it with her blood. She then heard a small dog barking, his paw was bleeding badly. *The blood must be his,* she thought. She bandaged the paw and was happy she was alone no more. Luna and Rusty became the best of friends.

Olivia Midelton (9)
Stratton Primary School, Stratton

PHOEBE'S SPOOKY HALLOWEEN

Once there was a little girl called Phoebe. She was excited because it was Halloween night. She was just about to go trick or treating when a skeleton ballerina dressed in cobwebs and spiders kidnapped her and took her to her room. Then she taped her to the wall and left her.

A few hours later, her mum came up, terrified, hoping she would find her daughter. She found her, untaped her and gave her something to eat and drink. From then on, she decided to never go trick or treating on her own in the dark again!

Eliza Rose Colwill (9)
Stratton Primary School, Stratton

THE ABANDONED TREE HOUSE!

Many mystical moons ago, in the time of black and white, everything was gloomy. On the edge of a rugged cliff stood a crooked and abandoned tree house. Where did it come from? Nobody knew who built it or how long it had been there.

One day, a group of friends were playing on the clifftop, the youngest of the friends was curious and wanted to go in. She reached the handle apprehensively and it fell off in her hands. As she turned away, she heard a creak and screamed as a shadow appeared at the door...

Sophie James (8)
Stratton Primary School, Stratton

THE STORYTELLER

On a hill, there was an abandoned castle. Nearby, in a little village, there was a storyteller, telling of the one who dared to cross its threshold.
It began twelve years ago! A foolish boy called Eric was in the castle when a zombie fell through the roof and dragged him to the top of the tallest tower. The zombie dropped him out of the window. He fell and got caught on a sconce. He realised he was going to die so he wrote his tragic tale and made it into a paper plane and sent it to his family.

Rhys Price (8)
Stratton Primary School, Stratton

CAKE SPELLS

Once in Transylvania, there lived a scrumptious, yummy Halloween cake. It could only do one thing - spells! Spells of anything you could think of.

One day, a little pug came from Dream World. Its tiny eyes had never seen such a spooky place! When it saw Cake, it wanted to eat it! Cake said, "No!"

He didn't want to be eaten!

Cake said, "I will grant you any spell of your dreams."

But the pug kept licking Cake. Cake just granted the pug a wish anyway.

Abigail Healy (9)

Stratton Primary School, Stratton

THE DEEP, DARK WOODS

It was a nippy Sunday morning, there was a boy called Tom. Tom decided to take a stroll in the woods.
While in the woods, he came across lots of spiders and spiderwebs. One of the spiders jumped out from a height and scared Tom. The spiders made a high-pitched noise and suddenly, hundreds more spiders appeared. They began to chase Tom. As he turned, he fell on a big stick and cut his face! He got up and started to run home as fast as his legs could. He lost the spiders and got home safe.

Paige Gliddon (7)
Stratton Primary School, Stratton

THE LOST VAMPIRE!

One day, a vampire called Lily lost her very clever and spooky mum when they were playing spook-and-seek. Lily searched everywhere around the forest but where could she be?
The next day, Lily was still trying to find her mum but she couldn't find her, so despite that, she didn't give up and kept persevering. Then. when she came back out, Lily heard creepy rustling sounds. Suddenly, out from behind the bushes jumped... Mum! Then they went inside and ate spaghetti and eyeballs.

Caitlin Brown (8)
Stratton Primary School, Stratton

ANNA'S BASEMENT TERROR!

One day, Anna and Alex were looking for Halloween outfits in Granny's basement. Then they stumbled across some potions in the cupboard. The potions and very weird and scary names like 'Eye of Newt' and 'Frog Spit'. Suddenly, Granny appeared behind them which gave them a fright! They screamed loudly. Granny said, "What are you doing with my Halloween decorations?"
For a moment there, Anna thought Granny was a real witch that flew on a broom and cast horrible spells! Granny explained that she had these decorations because she used to throw the best Halloween parties when she was younger!

Amira Perkins (8)
Werrington Community Primary School, Yeolmbridge

A REAL STAB IN THE BACK

There was a bang! Peyton couldn't resist, she had to see what was going on. She walked into the classroom and saw...
"Arghh!" she screamed.

Her best friend looked like she was possessed - blood everywhere, windows and doors opening and closing.
I'm going to die, Peyton thought to herself as she saw her friend coming closer. She ran as fast as she could but didn't close the door. Even though Peyton was running, her friend still caught up and did one of the worst things ever. Peyton was lying on the floor with a bloody knife in her back...

Mia Sergova Stoyanova (10)
Werrington Community Primary School, Yeolmbridge

YoungWriters
Est. 1991

YOUNG WRITERS INFORMATION

We hope you have enjoyed reading this book – and that you will continue to in the coming years.

If you're a young writer who enjoys reading and creative writing, or the parent of an enthusiastic poet or story writer, do visit our website **www.youngwriters.co.uk**. Here you will find free competitions, workshops and games, as well as recommended reads, a poetry glossary and our blog. There's lots to keep budding writers motivated to write!

If you would like to order further copies of this book, or any of our other titles, then please give us a call or order via your online account.

Young Writers
Remus House
Coltsfoot Drive
Peterborough
PE2 9BF
(01733) 890066
info@youngwriters.co.uk

Join in the conversation!
Tips, news, giveaways and much more!

YoungWritersUK @YoungWritersCW